January 2022
ISBN-13: 979-8-9855592-1-7
Photo Credit: Robert Cherone, 1987

COLLECTED POEMS

BOOK ZERO

JEFFREY CHARLES
KINARD

1986-1999

To all my friends, living and dead
I am better having known you.

Book Zero

[High School 1986-1989]

Between the desert of uncertainty 3
It's so cold and I'm so old 3
Another nobody 4
Fucking blood meat puppets 4
Blasting 5
See how limber he is 6
These are the outposts. 6
Chase me.. 7
Under the stars 8
Each man is a way.. 9
Damp 9
Fools and Wisemen! 10
You should never 11
While pushing to paint 12
Tell me once more 12
Down here... 13

[After School 1990-1991]

[EAST COAST 1992-1993]

[MAUI 1994-1995]

[MAINLAND 1995-1996]

[Vegas Santa Rosa 1997-1998]

[Capo Beach 1999]

BOOK ZERO

[HIGH SCHOOL 1986-1989]

Between the desert of uncertainty
and the forest of your mind
flows a golden river
memories of all kinds.
No one wants to go there
for the passage seems unsure
and everything that comes from there
is nothing but a blur.

*   *   *

It's so cold and I'm so old
My hands are turning blue
Voices soothe. I can't move
Keeps me from killing you

I can't wait the bits of hate
Clouding in my mind
I want to go but you know
I was left behind

*   *   *

Another nobody
screaming from his dusty corner
    of the world.
Another voice
joining the blizzard of noise.
Babbling animals
    discussing themselves
     to a wall of cackling
         nothing.

*   *   *

Fucking blood meat puppets
behind the garage
Warm water thrashing
with unknown life
    & creation promises

Atomic galaxy
Synchronicity
Licking the moonchild's
    paling fingers
               wanting to give her breath

*   *   *

4

Blasting
Pumping into motion
Mind expands
with bright explosions
Crawling melting
hanging on with shadows
     limp with heat
         and spilling sweat.

Imagine
Ponder drowning souls
breathing water
We never blink.
     I can't afford to miss
         a moment.

Lost
Confused
Stumbling wildly
into darkness.
Stars Prevail
Engines fail
     Crashing into bliss
         Unconsciousness.

*   *   *

See how limber he is
Muscles like moist chicken
See how he smiles
   arranging himself
      in grotesque positions.
Lingering in the shadows
hair in his eyes.
Figure in black
   dark acrobat
      steal a kiss for me, too.

*   *   *

These are the outposts.
Tidepools at dawn
Waking in the morning
gentle sun.
Basking like turtles
in the wasteland.
Singing like nightbirds
telling lies.

*   *   *

Chase me
into spiny woods
and starry nights
Watch for my smile
in the frosty moonlight
Search only for me
What I yearn
What I need
Discover me waiting
at the end
of my footsteps
Follow me here
to wherever I am
I need you to chase me
I need you to play
Please solve my puzzles
I will be all yours
if you'd only
find me...

*   *   *

Under the stars
  In tea leaf rivers
    Ponds of lowland
      Jungle creatures
        Bellow cries to the wind.

Old dry mudlands
  Crack and peel
    Under hooves of
      Creatures running shrieking
        Daylight on their tails.

The sun spreads yellow
  Brightness on the hills
    The sky explodes
      Waking the death of night.

While the watcher
  In the canyon
    Sits with flies evil
      Wonders what words
        Are on the wind.

        *   *   *

Each man is a way
Each birth
the birth
of a new way of life

*   *   *

Damp
Slipping deeply
Sweating
Pumping and grasping
Gasping and breathing
Blinking and squinting
Convulsing
Bursting into cooing
     and leg pain

*   *   *

Fools and Wisemen!
Near oriental bamboo forests
always moist and stiff
who gnaws with smiling mouth
the warm strips of flesh creatures
Skins peeled from still writhing bodies...
A shot of snake blood.
Oh, how he imagines
his groin fill with potency
from phallic meals.

Then enchained
leatherbound women
squirm on wood stages
Mixing blood and sweat.
Mesmerized by sadistic beating,
his pants grow full and warm
at thoughts and visions of rape.

Home – and his wife
greets him with a dry kiss.
Within him growls a beast.
Hand encloses her weak arm
The blood races – so hot.
He laps her dark skin.
He puts her to the floor.
He...

*   *   *

You should never
fall in love
with a guy like me.
I'm hooked to the fever
The light-headed heat
Crazy, you see, I've snapped.
I know what's out there.
I've seen sustained glimpses of...
        I've been it.

Madness.
It's freedom and I love it.
Like a droplet shining
    on the edge of a leaf
            I've fallen and rolled
                with the morning mist.

*   *   *

While pushing to paint
the universe,
play out dreams
in spontaneous scenes,
write secrets in symbols,
beckon four forces
with dancing,
compose with gods
the songs of angels
and demons...
I almost forgot
where I was.

*   *   *

Tell me once more
what you plan to do
at that old woman's house
Pierce my ears
Play games in the hall
Hide with children
in itchy bushes
    awaiting the switch

*   *   *

Down here
in the desert
people scour about
    the mirage
scooping for
    cool refreshment
Each time
disappointed
with a mouthful
    of sand.

*   *   *

[AFTER SCHOOL 1990-1991]

Dirt of the earth
people. Real humans.
Thin and relaxed.
Balding heads
on slouching necks.
Lined faces
Laughing and grim.
Gesturing loosely
to each other
in worn shoes.

*   *   *

The children
know where we are
Peddling bikes
under the bridge
smiling, riding
down the sidewalk.
But I'm lost.
Lost like a billion
  wandering souls
Wanting solace
Directions
Entertainment...

*   *   *

There is no method in this madness
There is a tunnel full of light
Freaks vying for attention
and beasts prowling in the night

There are legions unaccounted
There are wonders yet arrived
There are spirits in these dry bones
that yearn to come to life

If only for a moment
If only to explode
If only for a glimpse
of life and the road

*   *   *

Laugh and dance
into a trance
Let the words
collapse around you.
Hold the thread
until the end
Knowing your death
to guide you.

*   *   *

I knew her name once
On a night
A view like this
With the twilight
Liquid blue
Stars and
The moon.
Delicate clouds
Swirls dancing
Before the light
On a night.

We kissed against
The sacred tree
Bathed in blood
And the mystery
Unfolded
As to where
Did you go?

*　　　*　　　*

From a long moist trip
she comes to me
Tattered and twitching wings
she arrives on the sill
To remove a wet mask
warm her wings in the light
on other nights like tonight.

＊   ＊   ＊

What a liar
Talking trash
Gift of gab
Stretch of truth
Homing in on
What he wants
Running trouble
Wanted man
Conning you

Horseplay
Around the ledge
Flicking danger
Leaning leer
Draped in bruises
Cursed blessings
Summon storms
And lust of beasts
Shoved under

＊   ＊   ＊

She left me in the bug house writing
pot snap feeble coffee house scrawl
with my back against the wall.
Chickenscratch notations
waiting for the call
of my angel...
Pulsing through me like love
Rinse away this fear germ
with your light from above
Shine upon me...
I need your love and light
Make me feel alright
Shine upon me!
Come on...
Well, what are you waiting for?
Hello?

*   *   *

We meant to mean something
We tried to become.
I dabbled in everything
Looking for something.
To believe in fools
Is the magic of fools
To believe in nothing is mine.

*   *   *

Long ago
my friends and I
had nothing—
Empty handed
babes in the world.

We did school
and love
and drugs
and travel.
I experienced life—
Sucked it in
to fill the void.

The free
stroll thru life
with empty baggage.
Look hard enough
and you'll see...
Their feet
seldom brush the earth.

*   *   *

[East Coast 1992-1993]

Who me?
I'm not from around here
This is clear
No one speaks to me
In familiar tones
With friendly gestures
Smiles and eyes
Wondering
Maybe
If I'm the one who will

*   *   *

Hardly Sunday
The blood takes over the rhythm
Hearts follow steps to the moon
The head heavy
Can talk yet can't walk
The past pours into the future

Let's pretend
Time never existed at all
Til all the creatures
Find themselves
Crawling the walls

Back to California
Back to nothing at all
Let us be like
Creatures scratching
The paper off the walls

Sometime soon
In a tiny room
The blood will rule
The rhythm
And the dance will
Make a fool
Into a king.

*   *   *

Inches away
He thrashed
He sways
Life of skin
On the dark earth
He's risen
Still missing
A woman who might
never leave him alone

And his nights
Reach new heights
Like shuttles
But it just the bottle
Gripped confidently
in hand

*   *   *

On the road
with the timeless poet
Using words
I know are not mine
These symbols
leak from a black pen
into common prisons
Where definition
and interpretation
scratch the boundaries
into the world.

*   *   *

I was pacing
replacing
erasing
much hasting
to rise and fly.
I was drunken
flunken
heavy and shrunken
when I wanted to try.

*   *   *

I'm not feeling
very much today
Haven't got too much to say
Looks like my pretty
singing bird
has flown away

*   *   *

I know life
as a play of forces
And I learn
to be though becoming

*   *   *

The walls too close
The curve's too tight
Hit the breaks
I'm scared

*   *   *

Doin' the drifter
Change of scene mood lifter.
Look in the car next to you
Me and my fine sister
Off on another adventure.
Don't know where
We're going.
Don't think 'bout
Where we've been.
I've seen this all before
But don't remember when...

Doin' the drifter
Becoming a master
Jack of all trades
Not sure what I'm after.
For now this sunset
For now horizons
And endless laughter
At what it matters.
I still have a half tank of gas...
I think I'll pass.

*   *   *

[MAUI 1994-1995]

Would you wait another moment?
Would you waste the time to make
much to do
and barely the box open?

Can a step be hard to take?
Have you any questions?
Could there be any mistake?

There is no choice to make
but to move on
or wait.

*   *   *

To the islands
where the sky is smooth blue glass
From a cabana rooftop
someone recognizes you
as a gatherer
    of energy
    of experience...
We trade trinkets.

*   *   *

She is so sad
Built her dream too big
When reality comes
She looks at the gap
'tween what she wants
And what is.

She is so sad
Like an old song
Her father played
Like an innocence
That has been gone now
For so long.

She is so sad
Her sorrow rests
On her elbows
Upon the windowsill
And if you look up
You can see her still...
She is so sad.

*   *   *

When the sticky
  papaya juice of summer
soaks your sheets
creeping through
the open window
    and the sky is deep blue
  in the white light
of a harvest moon
Make slow love
on the backyard lawn
Until mother
  creeps up on you
    like a hungry squirrel.

*   *   *

Wearing black dress
    and stockings
High heels
She was waiting
Smiling as I gathered
    her slim September figure.
I had her
    against the dresser.
If she goes
I know I'd miss her
Bright eyes
    and bawdy whisper.

*   *   *

Stars beyond the palm
sand slips through fingers
forever gone.
Eternally away
the grasp invites
the bird to flight.
The sun undoes
our quiet night.
But it's alright
for now
we're here again.

*   *   *

Evening tormented
the fevered brow
The sweat of moments
lost somehow.

The evening presented
roses and scented
them with the honey
milk of frost and dew.

And evening promised
life now and new
from the change and circle
fragment futures
we smile as we pass through.

*   *   *

Toss in a frenzy
On your horse
Wild and lengthy
For the evening
Is nearer
And the moon
Is still full
In the meadows
Where love grows
And pants
Spurting seeds
To skies
Full of gods
And tropical roses
Rattle on the sill
Of the window
As we ride.

*   *   *

Come around
In the morning
In the morning
With the breeze
And the sun soft and shocking

Wake me slowly
From my dreaming
Form my dreaming
Warm and lucid
Like the birdsongs at dawn.

*   *   *

Touch me
Grab me
Reclaim me
Come to me again.
I love you
Beautiful
Precious
Sun jewel
Shining eyes
Bouncing curls.
Catch me by surprise again
My lover
My best friend
Reach me
With your awe and wonder
Quench me
With the spell you're under.

*　　　*　　　*

I carry with me
objects to remind me
where I have been.
I feel I am still there
        somehow...
I left something there
standing in my footprints.
As I continue onward,
I am unraveling.

These objects I carry
hold the essence
of what I have to remember.
All my memories
are leavings.

*   *   *

She changes
    more than just her mind
She improves
    Yearning to be more
        as you do.
To be everchanging
    Transforming
Would you stop her?
    Smash her cocoon
        for fear of losing her?
A far better experience
    to see a caterpillar change
        into a butterfly...
Then to own a frustrated worm.

*   *   *

[Mainland 1995-1996]

I am young
Rediscovering
What so many
Have realized before.

I, like a hunter,
Following tracks
In the snow
From long ago.

I get the feeling
Each time
I discover novelty
That those before me
Have moved on
From here.

*   *   *

We're free You're free I'm free
I love you and we're free
Free to dig up old crazy bones
Slip sideways down streets
In a haze or curl up in
Snug beds alone the sound
Of traffic and nightbirds around
Free to lift the vault of sky
And look up the togas of gods
Free to stick toes in mud
Find fairies sleeping
On moist moss so beautiful
Too small and I love you
Whoever you are or become
I love your becoming
I can hang with you and look
Crazed into your eyes
You won't flinch
'cause we're free like
All things are free
And wouldn't hurt a thing

*   *   *

Capture a moment
Ride along slowly
Dance with another
Under the covers
Recall the moment
Like any other

When two danced before
Down by the shore
Smell the scents
Of clean virtue
Gather around you
Dodging to kiss you
Falling to greet you

Secret still yearning
Wonder at the mirror
Sitting before you
She plays cards
She looking at you
Knowing you are...
Somewhere else.

*   *   *

So where did the love go
Out the window
Like a hobo
Skipping away
On a moonbeam
In a daydream
Did love run away?

And how will the love know
When she's lonely
And he's tired
Will it come back
And be inspired
By the downpour
And what's not washed away?

*   *   *

In his frazzled last appearance
words twirled from lips
of blood and water.
Her last regard was for a ghost
dancing thoughtfully away
in the long green grass
of her mind.
For a moment her eyes flashed
like sunshine off broken glass
Until, at last
she was a mirror in a dark room.

*   *   *

How clever we are
to keep from discovering
who we are.
How talented
at maintaining
our illusions.
Watch how quickly
I elude truth.
I use such cunning
to slip from responsibility.
The power of creation
I employ to rearrange
my reflection
in mirrors.
How brave am I
to remain so changeless.
How strong am I
to hold this all together
and pretend I am real.

*   *   *

Rounding a corner
he loves her and lets her
be as a warm summer breeze.
Sometimes like lately
he seems like a creature
grabbing up towards her knees.
But she is like sunlight
He knows life is just right
She blows the angle off with a sneeze.

*   *   *

Eyes bright
Sunlight
A golden halo
behind her head
I squinted
Felt a little sleepy
from soaking up the summer
and dreaming
Wondering who
warmed my belly
and hummed
a sleepy song

*   *   *

Tangled flight
And flutterfly
Stars spread thin
Across the evening sky
Today I heard your laugh
And had to sigh.
Somehow I'm led
To believe
You so tired
Chose to leave
Snapped the tether
And flew free
From the dream
I so eagerly
Still believe.

(EJD – 5/14/72 – 12/18/95)

*   *   *

Splintered
Shattered
Onto the ground
Our rock floor
With our narrow views
Waiting for our thoughts to fuse
We barely see what we're soon to know
It shows around the edges
Like a battered suitcase
Leaking clothes

*   *   *

Coming to life
in the after all
Knowing the dance
of the trip and fall
I've eaten the peach
of the close to death
Rose from the depths
to take a breath
On the water stands
the ones who go
Smiling like children
I've always known

*   *   *

She is unknown
        to herself
And we are all
        invisible to her.
Still, she wonders
    with us and laughs
            like she knows
                who we are.
She is mingling
    like a leaf in a courtyard
Tumbling on the breeze
    pouring thru the open gate.

                *   *   *

A single flame climbs higher
From the living chaos of the fire
Licking towards the icy stars
Dancing in the night air
Disappears...

I dreamt this morning
Of an old man
Tremendous hands
Cupping sand
And for all his strength
Power and might
Even he could not keep
His fingers woven tight.

                *   *   *

I release you
    and I'm free
I forget who
    I think you are
and I come to
    myself.
I crowd my theater
    with words
and I become
    lost in a dream.

This morning
the breeze drifts
    towards the wide
        naked sunrise.
And I abandon
    the remnants
        of a cold and
           lonely silence.

*   *   *

We pretend
Tell lies together
Want so badly
     To believe
What we think
     Is what we see.
I catch the glimmer
     In your eye
A moment's pause
     And a sigh.
We nearly remember
     We are actors
But then like fools
     Fall back in
               The slipstream
                    Of our mind-made roles.

*   *   *

I'm so free
Light in the clouds
Released.
Sometimes I long
For the gravity
That nearly pulled me in.
Love, you nearly had me.

*   *   *

43

What's that?
Skittering along
Like an alley cat
Gathering smiles
Stepping on cracks
Charmed, I'm sure
Charged, unleashed
Playing tricks and
Picking up treats.
Mixing into the current
Expounds, gets down
Lets it all fall out
Whenever found.
Dropping hints
A bit out of reach
Foolproof, aloof
Nothing to preach.
Wandering
To the heart of things
Tagging behind
Whatever life brings
And can sing
With fingers and toes
The tip of the nose
The beat of the rhythms
Vibrate the bones.
Inside-out
Interstellar probe
Like a beam of light
Don't think we're ever
Going home.

*   *   *

Where yer dreams send you
Where yer coaxed over the edge
Where you wonder where you are
What you've become

Where yer masks are useless
Where yer training fails
Where you have no more vision
What's still to come?

Where the weather spins
Where the world unglues
Where yer dreams send you
What wicked marvel

*   *   *

Well, it's a long way
from here
to there
And it's a long time to care
If I make it home again
If I see you
long lost friend
Somewhere on the road
without end

*   *   *

Could have slipped away
with the instant
Touched existence
Rode the golden road
back to oneness
But with my fondness
for what I am now
I'll be around
to watch
as the whole thing
comes down

*   *   *

[Vegas Santa Rosa 1997-1998]

Let's just hang out
drink coffee
be nice to each other...
What we did's
like playing with fire
making us flustered
making us liars.
And all those steamy
 silly words
spill like milk
then spoil and curd.
Not that we never
 felt that way
when feeling fresh
with flirt and play.
We're tickled quick
with tongues of flame
Say the look
and give some game
Then run
or have to smother...
Let's just hang out
drink coffee
be nice to each other.

   *   *   *

47

The greasy Romeo
was putting the move
on a couple college girls
Explaining to them
in his deep seductive voice
how important it is to him
to stare deep into
a woman's eyes
during sex.
That THAT was
the connection
he longed for...
To gaze into her soul
as he made love to her.

The girl seemed
interested
Not fooled
But like it was
the best she would hear
on a Sunday night
She smiled
like impressed.

Romeo glanced to me
and said, "Don't you think so, friend?"
I said I wouldn't know
I'm a buttfucker.

*   *   *

The young Swedish woman
dealing blackjack in Vegas
flirted with me a bit
and said I reminded her
of Dorian Gray.

I'm blond
and thin
and 27
Still get carded for cigarettes
Told I look maybe 22.

I like to fill their
nodding heads with nonsense
about drinking from
the fountain of youth
in St. Augustine
Which I actually did

with Eric.
We split a paper cup full.
Eric's dead now
and Dorian Gray
was rotten on the insides.

I told the Swede
"That's not funny."

*   *   *

Kiss me again
with your smooth
morning breath
I leave you in moments
    to return or for death
Do not dare to sleep
    through the dawn
Collect our new knowledge
    and carry on.
Know between us
if our ties are strong
Fate will connect us
in time or beyond.
Remember to no one
do we belong.
Dance for your rhythm
Sing for your song.

*   *   *

Once my angel
Once my friend
A kiss of death
And so love ends
For all of us who
Once dared pretend
That life is blessed
For all who bend

Kiss her once for me
I may not see her light again
She was once my angel
She was once my friend

*   *   *

I loved lonely
I beat beauty down
Crushed love underfoot
Feasted on kindness
To spit important
Seeds of desperation

I loved lonely
I was different
I was special
I built my world of ashes
Polished all my shadows
Glared from behind my hair
And never cared
I loved lonely

*   *   *

Float by
great thin man
through the needle eye.
Drift into life
Drift out again

Breathe we
simple refugees
from a far-off place
where we know each other.

I like the way
we mingle
on the tides
and dance on the sand
like foam.

*   *   *

Motion kicks
the slick still mix
and moves the steady groove
I had two eyes yesterday
Had a pocketful of words to say
Today I'm all ears
I feel I'm the dangler

Don't know what
Holds me up
Don't know what
Moves me

I dance on the end
of an invisible string
And no matter
where I find myself
I'm still dangling

*   *   *

Your dance
Shapes space
Moves the room
Lifts drunk spirits
From flesh bound tombs.

*   *   *

Gimme smoke
and gimme mirrors
Landscapes where
my dreams can smear
Where I can explode
and disappear
With spark ignite
my gasoline brain

*   *   *

Wonder why you bring all your smiles to me
I see myself sitting to casually
Not reacting – disembodied
I am a cactus
on this dessert tray
An uncomfortable joke
at the funeral of a dear friend
The guy with his eye on the sheer end
And master of worlds pretend
You're a wide-open flower
as far as I can see
Perhaps love on the brink
of tragedy....
And I wonder why you bring
all your smiles to me.

*   *   *

I'm tired
This life that drags on
Who I am desires
to collapse in a yawn.
Recoil from toil
The aching stretch
Kiss her once more
and annihilate death.

I'm tired
This struggle
to rise and remain
Find soft-skinned pleasures
and ignore the pain
Of a thought that lingers
like a curl of smoke
On the bonfire ashes
of my last childish hope.

Tonight, I retire
I quit – Won't go on
I pinch my eyes shut
and point for beyond.
I'm a wreck of a man
My deeds all undone
I smile for the sight
A new day
A warm sun.

*   *   *

Yearning for
the one last great strive.
Secretly praying for death.
When the tether snaps
and I go bolting away
Released from
pointless spinning
never anywhere
always
Bent forward for beyond
Racing to horizons
Wanting.

And always almost
Never enough
I can feel the heat of it
Stretching towards it
Never there
Always here
reaching for there
in some strange impossibility
of not knowing where I am.

*   *   *

Windows wide in my house
waiting for a breeze
To lift me from my sleeping pose
into other worlds of dream.
I do my work before me
Save my energy
For the journey on the wind
which blows across the sea.

I feel a little haunted
by all I have set free
The best I have given
as an offer to the sea
I know far away
in the distance that's to be
I hear upon the winds
what I love call to me

Soon I will be going
I'm already on my way
To find the eyes
that wait behind
everything I say
I can feel the beacon
pulsing stronger in my feet
To join again
my dear friends
that make my life complete.

*   *   *

Remnants from another life
Crowd my closet not my eyes
Relics boxed and stored away
I'm surprised they task my memory

Dust does make the sparkles dim
No polish wants rekindle them
Blank the wonder from my eyes
Blank to know the feeling died

Still don't know how a thing
Is drained of every potent meaning
Where was it that line was drawn?
The point when I could not go on

So much love now so much stuff
Used to mean the two of us
So many words now so much space
Where sound dissolves and love's replaced

*　　　*　　　*

What'cha gonna do
When your life is strife?
When you and your lady
Only fuck and fight?

What'cha gonna do
When it's not love?
And no genie appears
No matter how you rub?

What'cha gonna do
With the memories?
And the precious sparks
Of how it used to be?

What'cha gonna do
When you find someone else?
And you can't shake the feeling
You are more yourself?

What'cha gonna do
When you meet around town?
And your lips want to speak
But they haven't a sound?

It's so sad
The way two thousand days
Wind down.

*   *   *

For all her dusty
pancake make up
and her devastating shine
She never flinches
at a facelift
Sex, hard booze
or time

She's a monster
in doll's dresses
She is hollow
like the divine
She is dry
of satisfaction
She is pleasing
yet unkind

She smiles
to see me coming
I arrive drunk
on bending wine
Not the drink
for toasting blessings
But the other
hungry kind

I speed racing
through the desert
Chase oasis
Never find
The beating of a
true heart
Or a glimmer
in her eye

*   *   *

On a blind curve
In a fast car
Gripping the wheel
The tires squeal
And there's no time
To wonder who you are

*   *   *

I would have rather
Tracked mule deer
Been chased by badgers
Eaten spotted fruit
But they cleared it all away
For television and video games.

Life has become
Pseudo-exciting...
I'm plagued with the boredom
Named technology.

*   *   *

63

Spiral of lies
Misconceptions
Subterfuge
Redirections
No one I've known
Dares the truth...
Revelations
Deconstructions

Taught the shame
Attract the lies
Little ones
With a thousand eyes
Grow and lose their fingerprints
Appear to be real incidents
You spot them
They're flawless

From the fear
Of being caught
Tangled threads
To messy knots
And no one bothers
To sort you out
Means who cares
Who you are

*   *   *

We survive this life
On the better deal
A pinch a smidgeon
You lie I steal
Always dive
To dodge the light
When it doesn't
Strike you right
You might seem
Famous

But all the eyes
You think are starring
Are your lies
Guarding wary
Making sure
Your mask stays put
Secure against
A real look

One to knock you
Naked
One to knock you
Stupid
One to knock you
True

*　　　*　　　*

These tangles
Tear skin from bone
As I crawl onward
Bloodsoaked

These days
Pummel me unforgiving
Strip all meaning
From what I'm seeing

These deaths
End the same way
What's left of me
Is shocked clean awake

*   *   *

Orbiting
The stale ideas
The common place
Away from here
Where life is true
And feelings flow
I wonder why
We ever go

Back to forms
To pain and sighs
The boredom waiting
For lies to die
Plunge me into
Dreams again
The endless sleep
When sleeping ends

You who trace
The world with eyes
Forget the words
And search the sky
For answers, reasons,
Alibis
Feeling vacant
Afraid to die

*   *   *

I remember love
Remember how it filled me
I felt like I was living
Breathing
The taking and the giving

I remember love
Remember how it ruled me
I thought that I was gifted
Uplifted
With destiny and mission

I remember love
I remember how it used me
Sacrificed my longing
For belonging
All yours for the asking

I remember love
Remember how it freed me
Shook me down and beat me
Love taught me
No one else completes me

*   *   *

Your glamour sparkles
    Not no more
Your marvelous feathers
    On the floor
Your novel starlight
    Fades away
All you are for me
    Shallow anyway

Where is the life
    I wove in dreams
All I've seen
    Merely steam
Teeth fall out
    And age begets
An empty room
    I never forget

Blow away my bones
    Who cares
Damned by life
    Tricked in mirrors
Slumped in a corner
    Finished here
Such is life
    A handful of years

*   *   *

The animal runs through us
And we begin to breath
The pulse unsettles us
With movement

Sleek glances
Quick like memory
The animal runs through us
And we bound

We have night eyes
When the flame blows out
Twitching birds
We graze the light

There is only one sound
For quickening beasts
The hum of lightning
Drawing near

These lives hunt for meaning
As a blindman seeks his face
We have always gathered...
Following the herds
Across the open scape

*   *   *

[Capo Beach 1999]

A handful of words
Before I explode
The pressure of fate
I've been holding the load
And now I'm slipping
Now my strength is gone
And I can't hold on
I can't hold on

My dreams are calling
Spirit spends me to go
A little bit further
Into the unknown
I'm not immortal
Yet something inside longs
And I can't hold on
I can't hold on

I don't know the wherefore
My mind a feeble toy
Amidst the spirit pushing
Cares not if I'm destroyed
I am an instrument
It's the singer of songs
And I can't hold on
I can't hold on

*　　*　　*

I found Pete
In a pool hall
Not far from
His mom's house
In Santa Monica.
Not really.
Nobody has seen
Or heard from him
In many years.

Sober but still wasted
Asked me
To buy him a beer.
Approached me
Like a dog
Been kicked too much.
I was surprised
When I recognized him.

He had always been
A sort of local hero.
The old gang
Still sits around
Tells stories
About the times
He got arrested
On morning glory.

The gang had
Taken to a native shrub
With sticky leaves
And pods full of seeds.
Pete discovered it.
The seeds were some strange
Raw hallucinogen.

Brewed the little devils
Into a chalky tonic.
Two hours later
No one could walk.
Four hours later
And guys are
Stumbling zombies
Navigating dreamworlds
In everyday spaces.

Awhile later you'd sleep
A couple hours
And wake up someplace
Thankfully blacked out
Cuz you'd done
Some really
Strange shit.
Then, the drug
Got interesting.

The next day
You'd be relaxing
Someplace reflecting
Watching TV and talking
To a friend
For a while.
Then there'd be a twinkle
Out the corner of your eye
And your friend is gone...
He was never there.

And it's disturbing
When it keeps happening.
Everything will seem
Normal.
You're watching
The scenery passing
Outside the car window
On a trip to Oregon
With George
Or Mike
Or Doug.

A bubble pops
And you haven't even
Left the garage.
That's about the time
You decide
Not to drive.

Pete got out of the house
Was roaming the streets
At 4 a.m.
Being another creature
He wouldn't remember.

While everyone else
Is climbing into the fireplace
Or falling down the stairs naked
Hunting for water
Cuz the tonic
Makes you dry down to your stomach
Thirsty as a motherfucker
Gagging on the pasty
Sour taste in your throat.
Pete's climbing
Some neighbor's
Windowsill.

The guy happens to be
Our old school principal.
He comes out his house
Sees Pete standing on the windowsill
Reaching up onto the roof
And says, "Hey, you!"
Pete goes, "Shhh. Quiet, man.
I'm getting a drink
Of water." And he
Continues to
Grope the eave.

When the cops arrived
Pete's chasing
A white ferret
Thru the guy's bushes.
Pete leaps out howling
Onto the sidewalk
Startling the cops who
Are ready to draw pistols
Until they realize
This kid's
GONE.

They sit him on the curb
And can't decide
If he's drunk
Or on something.
While the cops are
Laughing
Discussing it
Pete gets up
Turns around
And starts urinating
On the lawn.

One cop says,
"Git over here!"
Pete turns and tells him,
"Hold on, man,
I'm taking a piss."
His dick in his hand
Like he finally caught
That white ferret.

The cops took him home
To the address on his ID
And turned him over
To his parents
Like, "Is this one yours?"

Who later watched him
Talk to himself
In the mirror
For an hour.
Who watched him
Meticulously fold
His laundry and toss it
Piece by piece
Over his shoulder
Into a heap across the room.

Their son didn't
Make sense anymore
And they watched
Like confused dogs
Heads tilted to one side.

The gang still tells
Lots of stories
About Pete.
Still
No one's seen
Or heard from him.

Pete who
Smoked a sandcrab.
Pete who
Made up his own language.
Pete who
Prowled the crowd
Like a jungle cat.
He beat the drum
We all moshed to.

Pete is unforgettable.
An infamous legend.
A true character...
I'd say he still is.

I bought him three rounds
But never let on
That I knew it was him.
He told me tales
Of ordinary woes
And common frustrations.

I guess that's the other
Death of a legend.

*   *   *

Tragic it is
to live so poorly
in a beautiful place

There's a babbling brook
out the window
and week-old dishes
shipwrecked in the sink

There's a fresh breeze
in the thinning leaves
And the floors
are mysteriously sticky

The trash is overflowing
into smaller bags
And stale beer
mingles with the salt air
drifting up from the sea
like a kite

The fridge works hard
for condiments

Tragic it is
to live so poorly
in a beautiful place

*   *   *

Silly
Such a clown
Hope and love
And horse around
Play with words
Hang upside down
Dance with shadows
Dance with light
Gather stardust
Late at night
On the moon
Beyond the gate
Silly apes
Go on the make
To howl and hoop
The absolute
Absence of truth

*   *   *

I know how
to close doors.
To leave things
untouched.
I can abandon
all feeling
and draw inside
Turn locks
and hide.
I can divide.

I let birds
    fly away
Leave lovers
    with nothing to say.
I can grow cold
and forget love
    and life
            and never
                be hurt.

*   *   *

From sleep
I awake to realize
a thousand eyes
of the departed
watch me from the other side.
I am not nervous
in the breezy laughter.
I am not as here
as I thought I was.
And I am the one
who forgets
what I'm doing.

＊　　　＊　　　＊

Moments ago
I forget.
Hours ago
I've misplaced.
Years pass
And I let them.
I strive for
    The beginning
            Which is here
The moment
I forget
Who I've been
And what I hope
To become.

＊　　　＊　　　＊

My misshapen moon
My blurry eternity
Spinning in the darkness...
Or is that me?

My crowded starlight horizon
My clusterfuck reality
Drunk in the moment
Trust not what I see

I'm a quiver of ideas
Drawn back and freed
A mixed interpretation
Of sudden novelty

I'm climbing the corkscrew
I'm rounding the bend
Something might come back
But it won't be me again

*   *   *

This is not reality
This city...
These chairs.
Man cannot create
      Reality.
What is real
Has always been here
And is buried beneath
      This concrete street
            Full of cars.

*   *   *

Maybe now in retrospect
Another path I may confess
Would not have wrought
My heart such pain
But it's not mine to choose again

I have stumbled thru the night
Choosing what I thought as right
I've been tempted every turn
And by my wits this fate I've earned

I may decide it's to my merit
To persist, to grin and bear it
For I may find I'm wiser now
Illusions shed and more truth found

What are we who do not wait
To be sharpened by our fates
But boldly go we know not where
Into the night to cash our fare

Maybe now in retrospect
Another path I may confess
Would not have wrought
My heart such pain
But without scars, we have not names

*   *   *

Jeff, 16, Modjeska Canyon

www.ingramcontent.com/pod-product-compliance
Lightning Source LLC
Chambersburg PA
CBHW052153090426
42741CB00010B/2246